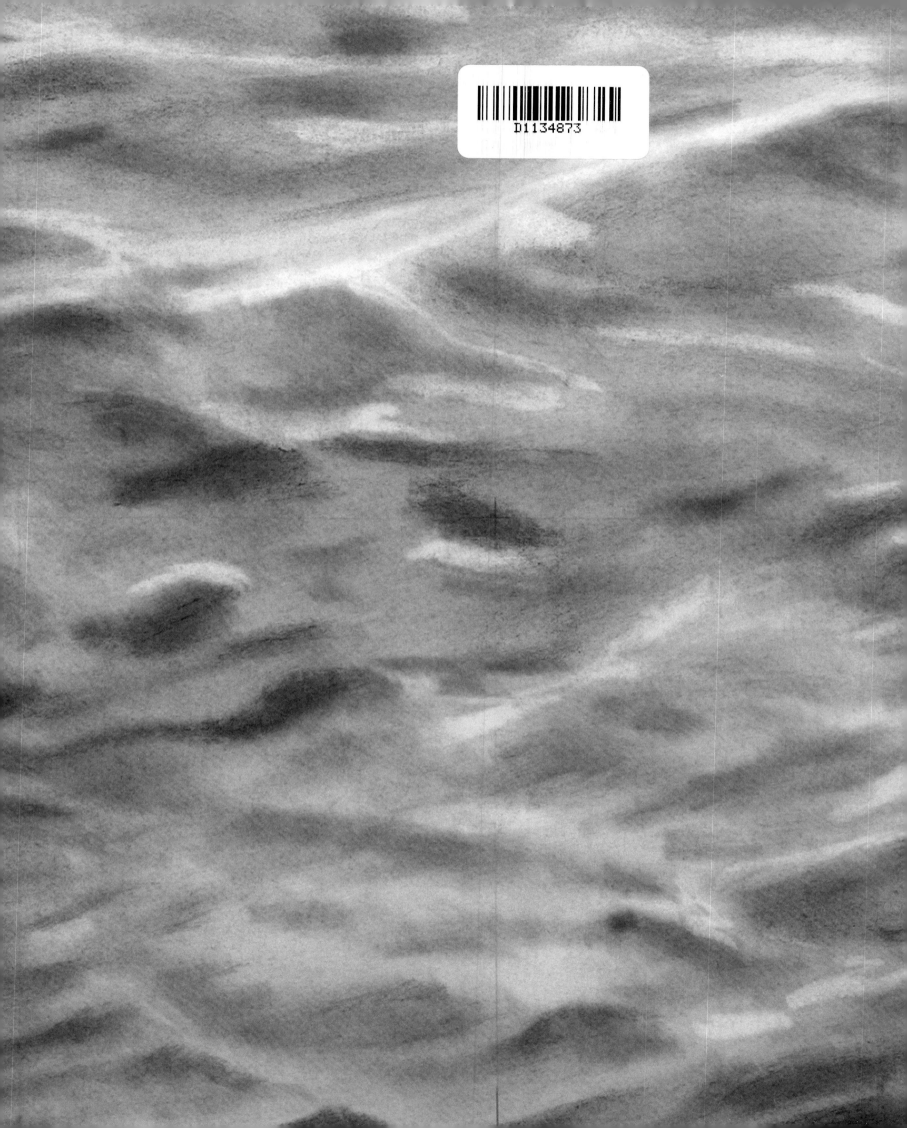

Golden Hands

Golden Hands

Drawings & Reflections by Rachel Feferman

Anderson-Lovelace ∘ Los Altos Hills ∘ 2009

In memory of
Helen Grand Feferman

For my parents
with love

Anderson-Lovelace Publishers
13040 Alta Tierra Road Los Altos Hills CA 94022

ISBN 0-9626372-8-9
ISBN 978-0-9626372-8-5

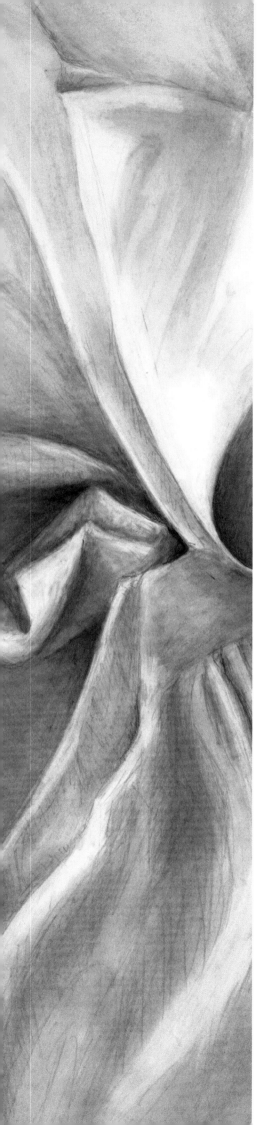

Contents

Introduction

In Poland, before the First World War, a Jewish girl trained to become a seamstress. She sewed an apron out of plain white cotton by hand. She carefully measured out the rows of pleats to decorate the bib and the hem of the skirt. Her tiny stitches were almost invisible. Because of her skill with a needle and thread, she was nicknamed *Gilde Manz*, or Golden Hands. After the war, she came to America.

That girl was Helen, my father's mother. When I was a girl she taught me how to sew, and when she left her last apartment in 1983, I inherited her green metal lunch box full of buttons and her apron. On my return home to Palo Alto, after helping her pack for her move to the Jewish Home for the Aged in Los Angeles, the lunch box set off the security alarms at the small Burbank airport. The guards opened the beat-up box only to find a jumble of old buttons in crumbling cellophane packets, unused snaps, and a bag of zippers cut from old clothes in order to be used again. I kept it all and brought everything with me when I moved to the Pacific Northwest in 1986.

One day, it was near the end of 1994, I took out her apron and drew it. After the first drawing, I did another. Working with pencil and powdered graphite, I drew the apron hanging, folded, twisted, from the front and from the back. I drew it small, as if from a distance, and close up. I loved the way light fell on the gathers of the skirt, articulating a rippling landscape of ridges and valleys. I drew it in combination with other things: an envelope, a loaf of challah, flowers, apples, a violin, and old photographs of my grandmother. I also drew it with barbed wire and piles of dead bodies.

Helen's apron was my touchstone, carrying me back across the century to the world of the old country. This world has all but vanished; the exceptions to this are far and few between. Her apron stands in counterpoint to the massacres of the Holocaust in the world that I drew, yet my grandmother herself was never in a concentration camp, nor was anyone else in my immediate family. In no way discounting the very real horrors suffered at the time, the Holocaust also left a hell of the human soul in its wake, which continues to haunt us more than sixty years later. The truth these drawings put forth is that, in slightly different circumstances, the dead bodies I portrayed could represent any of us. I titled these drawings "Golden Hands" in tribute to my grandmother. My original idea was to make one hundred drawings of the apron: one for every year of the twentieth century or every year of Helen's life. She died in 1997, just two months shy of her hundredth birthday. When I started these drawings, she had already begun to slip away, both mentally and physically.

At first I was flooded with ideas and often completed two drawings within a month. As the work progressed, the way I drew became more exacting and my output slowed down. The apron crumpled in the dark grass (Drawing 40) was the only drawing I completed in 1999. In August of that year, I was diagnosed with breast cancer, and my work on the series came to a standstill. There were forty-two numbered sheets of paper: thirty-two drawings were finished, the rest were in progress.

The ten months of cancer treatments passed outside of everyday time. I felt like a drowning woman and thought only of getting back to land, if land still existed. I disentangled myself from doing anything that made my life more difficult than it already was. This included letting go of my work on the drawings because of the weight of sorrow I felt while I was creating them. I had also lost my ability to concentrate, just like that. After the treatments were over, I felt half maimed and half newborn, full of wonder and stupor. My life was seemingly the same, but only on the surface. In many ways my load was lighter, for much was left behind. The box with the drawings sat unopened; I couldn't bring myself to look at them.

In 2006 I was re-diagnosed, this time with advanced breast cancer. The things I still wished to do came quickly into focus. I had always envisioned these drawings in a book, but this notion lay tucked away for some other day. I had procrastinated on the book project for the usual reasons—lack of time and money—but other reasons were more deeply buried. I was hesitant to expose my hidden world, and I worried about my grandmother's privacy. Didn't the dead, people who could no longer speak for themselves, have the right to be left undisturbed? I couldn't explain why I had combined images of my grandmother's apron, her face, and eventually her death, with piles of anonymous dead bodies and barbed wire, imagery associated with the concentration camps. Though the drawings had always made perfect sense to me, I was never able to answer these questions to my satisfaction. The best reply is simply: the images belonged together because I kept putting them together, like stars in the same constellation. Both creativity and grief are irrational, and most often inarticulate as well. The work on these drawings was formed by the impulses of my eyes and hands, and guided by an ache in my heart. Words followed later.

When we mourn, for one person or for many, we cry. And we praise life. Using whatever words or pictures we can find, we begin to piece together what we remember. My grandmother had a black silk scarf with large white polka dots, the size of nickels. As I stare at it, the white dots begin to rise. They are spheres hovering above a sea of black, which keeps every dot separate and unifies them all. I start falling into this endless space, and then I'm pulled back to the memory of her stylish scarf, with food spilled on it over breakfast. Sight is unstable. The dots continue to make lines, circles, and mazes. And what to make of the after-images, the phantom circles of darker black, flashing between the dots?

What I find keeps changing. Here are the drawings and my reflections about doing them. I hope they speak to you.

—Rachel Feferman, 2009

I dream about my grandmother's apron. It is with a packet of papers,
like letters, in a loose, untidy bundle tied together with ribbons. (July 7, 1996)

Imagine the dream continuing: I untie the ribbons and carefully begin to leaf
through the pile of papers. I have taken what I found: drawings, photographs,
and pages from my journal, organized the contents a little (like with like) and
shaped them into this book. I have done my best to stay true to my original
frame of mind. The apron, my handwriting, the pencil marks . . .
I hope you are able to find their spirit within these pages.

In the Studio

My ideal studio is a place where I can shut the door on the rest of the world for uninterrupted stretches of time. There is no phone and no computer. The room doesn't double in use for other purposes, such as classes, bookkeeping, or putting up guests. It's a place where I can walk away from the work midstream and find everything just as I left it when I return, mess included. It's spacious, quiet, and filled with indirect natural light. The dream studio itself is neutral, it's like a sheet of paper that I then charge with my work. But a real space isn't a blank slate, for rooms have personalities, and their arrangement dictates how we move within them. As I reconstruct how I made these drawings, I keep picturing my studio—for me the work is completely wrapped up with being in that room and being alone. In The Poetics of Space, *Gaston Bachelard wrote, "If I were asked to name the chief benefit of the house, I should say: the house shelters day-dreaming, the house protects the dreamer, the house allows one to dream in peace." Though a far cry from my ideal, my studio did just that.*

My room was on the second floor of a massive turn-of-the-century building in downtown Port Townsend. As studios go, it was neither big nor small, nearly twice as long as it was wide. It had a high ceiling that made it feel larger than it actually was. The old floorboards were painted a rusty red; the walls, already far from pristine when I moved in, were off-white. Two tall windows at the far side of the room faced south. The natural light changed dramatically throughout the day, and I paced my drawing to make the best use of it. For instance, if I wanted to see strong shadows in a still life, I worked on those parts of a drawing in the early afternoon. I hardly ever used the single bare light bulb that dangled from a cord in the middle of the ceiling. During the seven years I rented this studio, I never bought a shade for it or changed the bulb.

I did most of my drawing on three long worktables in the middle of the room; I also worked on the walls and the floor as needed. It was possible to hang six drawings in a row on the wall that ran the length of the room and to stack them three rows deep, although it was rare for me to put up that many drawings at once. On the far wall, between the two windows, there was a space just wide enough for a single drawing. A drawing hung on that wall occupied a special spot, set apart from the others.

The drawings in progress confronted me each time I entered the room. Sometimes I went straight to work, but there were other days when I needed time to switch gears. On those days, I might fool myself into acting as if I had no intention of getting any drawing done. I would make a cup of tea (when in doubt make another), pull a chair up next to the radiator, and stare at the trees lining the street. This radiator was part of the

5

original steam heating system and set on a master timer for the whole building. Twice a day in the cold months, it would start clanking and soon the room would be toasty.

When I had sufficiently gathered myself, I would put on my work apron and turn my attention to drawing. I listened to the same cassettes day after day. The music was like a hypnotic trigger: when it played, I worked. I would hear the first few measures, then barely notice that it was still on. It helped to quiet my thoughts and drown out the sounds of the noisy street below. Tourist season started early each spring and lasted until the worst weather drove people home. The warmer days also brought out the street musicians. The man who regularly claimed my corner of the building had three violin tunes he played. In summer I would open my windows and hear "Danny Boy" yet again. But the bulk of distractions slipped to the side, at least temporarily, when I was concentrating.

When I began the Golden Hands drawings, I wanted to return to the feeling-tone of an earlier body of my work, but this time with a more open-ended approach. In the 1980s I

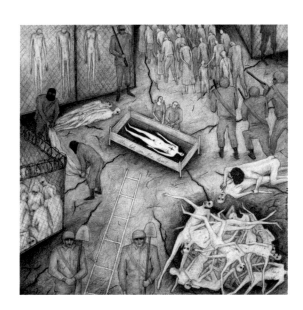

Hole in the Heart #2, 18" x 19", 1986

produced a series of small-scale narrative paintings and drawings. A number of these images are of fearful visions, such as the one in "The Hole in the Heart #2," where distorted bodies lie tossed in an open grave. I was able to work with the horror of my imagery by zeroing in on minutiae. By the end of the 1980s, my painstakingly detailed style felt too confining, and I moved on. I had little idea where my work would lead me next. I spent several years experimenting with other ways of drawing, and working with etching, linoleum blocks, and collographs. Printmaking made it possible for me to generate variations of a single image relatively quickly—this thrilled me. As I varied my techniques, my imagery broke away from the earlier narrative structures. By the time I began the Golden Hands series in 1994, my way of putting images together had undergone a sea change, yet the earlier themes remained within me, hungry for a voice. One way I carried these themes forward was to work with some of the same elements in the new drawings. From the very start, I combined the apron with images of dead bodies and barbed wire.

The paper I chose for the Golden Hands series was Arches 90-pound hot press, an archival paper, creamy white, designed for watercolor. I always want to run my hand across the smooth surface of a blank sheet, and a pencil glides across it easily. On a rougher paper, the pencil lead would bump across the tooth of the texture and break up the continuity of a line. This paper is just lightweight enough to trace a drawing from one sheet to another with a light source behind it, and at the same time it is quite durable, able to take vigorous drawing or erasing without tearing. The paper's surface changes as a drawing builds: erasing roughens it, dense pencil work creates a slippery sheen, while the graphite powder or fixative creates a fine texture.

I used many kinds of drawing pencils and would wear my favorites down to short stubs. Drawing pencils are gradated by the hardness of their lead; working with the softest/darkest of these pencils is like drawing with butter. I used graphite sticks and loose graphite powder along with the pencils. To soften the pencil work or manipulate the powdered graphite, I used rolled paper smudge sticks, rags, cotton balls, and Q-tips. White rubber erasers, some with rounded edges, others with squared-off edges, worked well for most erasing. For the most stubborn areas I used extra-tough erasers intended for ink.

As I think back, I am able to remember many details about how I did these drawings, yet the notes that follow are only my best guess. With the benefit of hindsight, the technical aspects of the process may appear almost mechanical, but the process wasn't nearly as clear-cut as my descriptions suggest: deliberation, trial and error, and interruptions—in other words, life—all figured in. Except when any of these had a direct bearing on the physical process of drawing itself, I have left them out of this account.

I began Drawing 1 by looking at the apron. I laid it out before me on the table, then tried hanging it from a coat hanger. I took my time until I found the arrangement I preferred. This step sounds obvious, but so much is decided before one ever picks up a pencil. Once the apron was placed to my liking, I was ready to draw. I started by blocking in the general shape of the apron with light, tentative lines. As the apron gradually emerged on the page, some of the lines became darker and I began to work on specific details, fitting the parts to the whole. While I drew, I asked myself a steady stream of questions, such as: Where do the edges of the apron fall in relation to the edges of the paper? Is the upper strap longer than the length of the bib? Does it look right when I draw it that long? What are the shapes in the space surrounding the apron? Most of this dialogue went on below the surface of my attention, just a part of hand-to-eye navigation.

Once I had captured the overall shape of the apron, I dusted the inside of it lightly with graphite powder, pressing a little more graphite

DRAWING 1, 30" X 22", 1995

into the center where the darkest creases fell. The apron shape now had an overall gray value. Then I moved on to the ridges of the gathers and the lines of the pleats, picking them out with an eraser. We tend to think that drawing consists of making dark marks on white paper and that erasing is a way to remove mistakes, yet an eraser can also double as a wonderful drawing tool, making it possible to lift light areas out of a dark ground. It wasn't long before I started switching back and forth between an eraser, a smudge stick, and the pencils.

As I draw an object, I feel a resonance with it—my mind holds the object, and the distance between it and myself is bridged with empathy. If I'm already attached to the object, as I was to the apron, this sense of connection is even stronger. The process of translating a three-dimensional object into two dimensions feels like I'm sculpting it on the page. The push and pull of pencil and eraser is physical. There is also a corresponding sensation of weightlessness and weight attached to light and dark areas, since visual principles make light shapes appear to expand and darker ones to recede, as in dark shadows.

When this first stage of the drawing looked right to me, I sprayed it with a workable fixative to protect the image from smudging while I worked on the background. "Workable" means you can continue to draw on top of it. It remains possible to erase lines once a drawing has been fixed, but it takes more elbow grease. Because spray fixative hardens in tiny droplets, marks made on a fixed drawing sit on top of the paper slightly differently from marks made on the more absorbent, untreated paper. Fixative applied at different stages throughout a drawing creates varying degrees of resistance, which helped me extend the range of tones.

I set the drawing I had fixed to the side and began to draw the background on another sheet of Arches paper. I tackled the bands of dead bodies first. As I worked out the position of each figure, I could feel an imprint of their limp weight in my body, even though they came out of my imagination. To my surprise, the dead bodies in the Golden Hands series were less contorted than those in the earlier drawings; they had gained weight and now appeared almost peaceful.

When I was satisfied with the way these bodies fit together, and before tracing them onto the first drawing, I made a cutout to protect the drawing of the apron. I traced the shape of the apron onto a piece of newsprint, cut it out, and tacked the cutout over the drawn apron temporarily. It fit precisely. During the messier work to follow I would be able to rest my hand on the cutout without smudging the apron, and the graphite powder would be confined to areas where I wanted it. This cutout would also give the edges of the apron a crisp definition. Next I taped the template drawing to the window. I placed the first drawing over it and traced the bands of bodies onto the background. After this, I moved the drawing back to the table, dusted the bands of bodies with loose graphite, then removed the light areas with my eraser, much as I had done when drawing the apron. I drew the most detail in the band at the bottom and progressively less detail in each band above.

I made another set of newsprint cutouts, this time for the shape of each band of bodies. When the drawing was entirely masked except for the open negative spaces, I went over the whole sheet with loose graphite, making a few separate passes to achieve the gradation from dark to light. I wanted the background to have a subtle feeling of rising.

When I needed to look at the drawing I would take off the cutouts—or just lift a corner to peek—then tack them back in place and continue, a carryover technique from printmaking. The drawing at this stage still seemed unfinished. What did it need? I thought about adding lines of barbed wire. I laid out pieces of barbed wire that I had collected, and again drew the lines of the wire on the template sheet first. After I had traced these lines into the background, I went over them a few times with a freshly sharpened pencil. I pressed as hard as I could, for I wanted the lines to carry the biting feel of the wire itself.

After I removed all the newsprint cutouts, I continued to work on the entire picture until it read as one whole. I was excited by what I saw. I had begun work on another full view of the apron, this time with the bodies decorating the border of the skirt (Drawing 2), even before this one was finished. From that point on, I always had a number of drawings in progress.

Months later, the body template that I used for the background of the first drawing became Drawing 12, where the pattern makes up the entire image. The rows of sewn-down pleats on the bib and the hem of the apron made subtle raised stripes in shades of white. These stripes show up clearly in Drawing 21. The pattern of Drawing 12 was striped too, only with stripes of bodies and barbed wire. I went on to use stripes in many of the other drawings: the bold black stripes in Drawing 33 of the violin and apron tucked in the case and the four long twisting forms in Drawing 19 are two quite different examples.

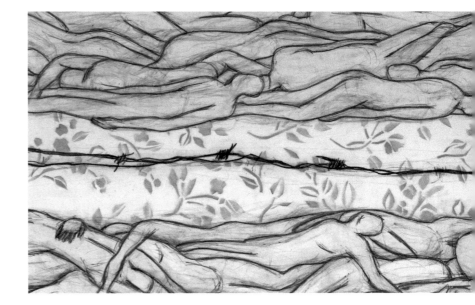

Even though the apron was made of plain white cotton cloth, it started me thinking about textile patterns, which I have always loved. Many patterns on fabric are of flowers and leaves, the natural world weaving through our clothes and homes. I used a traditional stencil technique to create the lacy flowers between the

DRAWING 12, 30" X 22", *detail*, 1995

bodies in Drawing 12. I cut the flowers out of large sheets of acetate with an Exacto knife, then rubbed loose graphite powder through all the little holes to the paper beneath. The acetate stencils were sturdy, and I re-used them many times. Sometimes I applied this pattern to a single area, such as on the cloth in Drawing 9, other times to the whole page.

It is an arbitrary choice to begin a drawing on a sheet of white paper. Sometimes that emptiness suited my purpose, but other times I wanted to start on a lively surface. I would prepare sheets of paper with patterns, graphite, or cross-hatching, beforehand. Creating patterns is often slow craftwork; it is repetitive and comforting to do. When I was working with something sad like the dead bodies, I could carry the work along without constantly feeling at the edge of my nerves. At the same time, the patterns broke up the surface of the paper in interesting ways. A pattern or texture on the paper gave me something to work with or to work against.

In Drawing 27 I drew the apron cradling several apples on a sheet of paper already covered with the pattern of bodies. There were no empty spaces between the bodies—it was like a wallpaper of the dead. When the drawing was finished, the bodies remained visible at the bottom of the page and receded behind the stripes at the top. Only an occasional line within the still life gave a clue that the pattern had once been there as well. Each of these places records my choice to accentuate, camouflage, or remove the original bottom layer. The pitcher in the upper corner of this drawing is patterned with birds and flowers. Later, I enlarged elements of its pattern on a full sheet of paper, then used the design in Drawings 28 and 36.

The flow of the imagery from one pattern to another, and between the patterns and the objects, was an ongoing conversation. A pattern, by definition, is based on repetition, and conceivably could go on forever. Objects, on the other hand, are singular, like the apron, or countable, like the number of apples in Drawing 27. We respond to some objects in particular, they seem to have an intimacy to them. We might talk about these objects having a soul—or is it our own?—reflecting back in our gaze.

My grandmother's apron was at the center of the drawings, regardless of whether it appeared in every single image. Soon after I began drawing it, I became curious about other objects that belonged with it. Since I thought of the work partly as a memorial, my questions expanded from "What can this apron tell me?" to "What do the dead want?" and "What things do the living want for the dead?"

The objects I chose—a pitcher with flowers, an envelope, pieces of barbed wire, apples, rocks, a loaf of challah, a violin—offered partial answers. Whether they were made by hand, by machine, or shaped by natural forces, they all have a history and are themselves indifferent. The story we give to them has everything to do with time measured against the length of our days. Some objects outlast us, while others, like the flowers, exist only briefly.

I found the squat pitcher on a high shelf in my friend Jane's kitchen. I was hunting for a nicely shaped vase for a still life. In my imaginary book of exceptional manmade objects, pitchers as a general category rank close to perfection. They are useful: to store or pour water, milk, or wine, and also beautiful: the balance of the handle and spout against the symmetry of the body is intrinsically pleasing. Lastly, a pitcher's surface is often decorated. The first time I drew this pitcher I left it plain (Drawing 14), yet its colorful design had been what originally caught my eye. The loosely painted birds and flowers were full of movement, a joyful declaration of life, and the pattern soon found a place in the drawings as well.

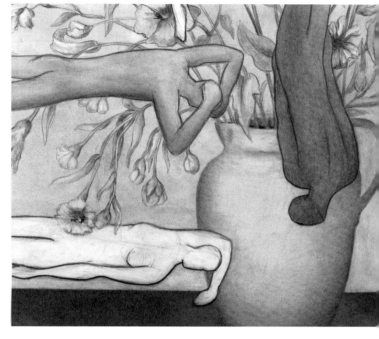

DRAWING 14, 30" x 22", *detail*, 1995

I used the pitcher to hold flowers. There was an organic farm stand in the middle of town that sold U-pick flowers from the field next to it. I picked many bouquets there, walking among untidy rows of cornflowers, poppies, dahlias, lilies, and many other kinds of flowers. It seemed as though the sky was always a vivid blue, and a storm was always about to come. At first I picked bouquets just to brighten the studio, but when I saw them next to the drawings, I knew they fit right in—flowers have always belonged with the dead.

A good bouquet, not the supermarket variety, is an assembly of delight. As I sit writing at my kitchen table, I am looking at the flowers that I picked yesterday, loosely arranged in a blue glass vase. Tucked among them, there are a few apricot-gold roses that are touched with rouge on the back of their petals. These colors bounce across to the creamy yellow of a different rose, also to a light orange daylily, striking a harmonious visual chord. Related in color, but with more pizzazz, the red-orange dahlias leap forward. Each dahlia has a ring of bright yellow pollen in the center, which surrounds a red so dark it almost appears black. The leaves and stalks, so many shades of green, set everything off; the flowers vibrate.

The bouquets for my drawings were equally colorful and I longed to capture their exuberance. I enjoyed drawing the radial and tubular flowers, the unfurling buds, and the shapes of the leaves, but this was one of the few times I was frustrated with the limitations of the graphite, for there was no way to include the brilliance of the colors. The short life of a cut flower was a more workable difficulty. As a flower wilted, I replaced it or improvised from my head.

After a tree flowers, the fruit begins to grow. God wants to tempt us, or nature to nourish us, and makes a sweet, round apple, just the right size to hold in the cup of one hand. Perhaps because I was thinking about a symbolic way to leave food for the dead, I drew the apples and also the bread. I often used apples and pears to teach my drawing students how to model rounded forms, and drew alongside them. The fruit seemed so human. Collecting the apples was simply a matter of a trip to the store, but choosing the best ones—beautiful, hard, and unblemished—involved a thorough examination of each and every one. One time a man stocking produce at Safeway couldn't make out why it was taking me so long to pick a few apples. He kept on asking if he could help me. With hindsight, the perfect comeback would have been: "Yes, do you have an apple I can leave out for months before it begins to rot? One so perfect in every way that Snow White will reach right for it?"

Drawing 21, *detail*, 30" x 22", 1996

One of my favorite jokes has to do with time, pleasure, and apples too. It goes like this: A salesman was traveling along a country road when he came upon a farmer standing underneath an apple tree with a pig in his arms. He thought this a peculiar sight, so he said: "Excuse me sir, but I couldn't help but be curious as to what you're doing." "Well, as you can see I am feeding the pig," the man replied. "Do you always hold the pig when you feed it?" "Well, he likes apples." "But doesn't that take an awful lot of time?" said the astonished salesman. "Yes, but what's time to a pig?"

Not all the materials were a pleasure to collect; the barbed wire was more nightmare and no levity. The pieces of barbed wire came from a fallen fence, half-buried by blackberry vines, in a field near my home. I had stumbled across it while walking my dog and when I wanted barbed wire for the first drawing I knew exactly where to find it. It was difficult to cut off pieces without getting hurt. My fears of handling it continued in the studio—even the small sections were menacingly well designed.

I wished for a way to include music in the drawings: the image of an instrument could conjure music on the silent page. A violin was the natural choice. Traditionally it has been an instrument of nomadic people, easy to carry, yet also of cultured people—the Jewish people (a sweeping generalization) are both. In the right hands violin music is as expressive as the human voice. My hands weren't particularly musical ones. I had taken violin lessons as a child, but they ended with the first wave of adolescence. From then on, the instrument remained familiar: it looks like a body with a waist and belly, and small scroll head at the end of the long neck. An acquaintance lent me an old violin to draw. Its beat-up case reminded me of a small suitcase dented with the traces of voyages. The voyage was always across the ocean.

I have lived near the beach and my image of the sea begins at my feet. I wanted to draw the sea that joins all seas. I couldn't bring the sea inside but I could collect rocks. I carried many granite rocks from the beach to the studio until I had a good-sized pile. They were heavy, with a roughened texture; the apple skins were thin and shiny, the barbed wire had little flakes of rust that chipped off every time I bent it. Finding and handling each of these things added to what I knew about them.

DRAWING 36, 30" x 22", 1997

The way I drew these objects changed over the years. A number of the later drawings involved fewer steps but took considerably more time than the first drawings. Drawing 36, with the apron spilling over the case, took countless hours. After I had drawn the violin, the apples, and the apron—and this was a long after—the contrast within the background overpowered the more nuanced rendering of the objects. At that stage the background was a flat positive/negative design, similar to the background in Drawing 28, with the large ear. I smudged graphite into the light areas of the background design and added many tiny pencil strokes on top of the graphite to get subtle gradations of tone. The surface of the background became quite rich. In one of those unintended reversals, the background continued to vie with the still life for the eye's attention, because all the additional work invested the negative space with an importance that hadn't been there earlier—although now I liked the effect.

Because the later drawings required a big commitment of time, I wanted to look ahead before I jumped into one of them. I often set up several still lifes before choosing the one I liked, and photographed some of them. The photos were a quick way to read an arrangement. I was interested in some of these still lifes, but it happened that I never chose to draw any of them, either from life or from the photo. I could have photographed the still life for Drawing 36 and drawn from the photo, but I didn't. It would have been another way to get to a similar, but not the same, drawing. My rule of thumb for when to use a photo was when the subject was difficult or impossible to draw from life: the portraits of my grandmother, the poses of the hands, the always moving sea, and the apron scrolls, all fell into this category.

It is interesting to compare Drawings 28 and 36. Drawing 28, of the large ear, was mostly done from a photo I took while my grandmother lay dying, while the apples, violin, and apron in Drawing 36 were drawn from life. The distinction is not something you tend to notice. You would be more likely to see that both sheets of paper are covered with a similar pattern, that there is a correspondence between the size and shape of the violin case and the ear, or to notice the bird trapped within the lid of the case, and which rises out of the top of the ear. The photo source is more noticeable in some of the portraits of my grandmother, where the quality of an old photo is part of the meaning of the image, for instance in Drawing 35.

DRAWING 35, 30" X 22", 1996

It is easier to create a realistic illusion when working from a photograph than from life. At its crudest this is considered copying, not invention. An image in a photo has already been flattened into two dimensions, the shapes and proportions don't wiggle. Drawing from life involves a perceptual shift from what we think we're seeing, to what we are actually seeing. Foreshortening is the simplest example: If you are facing a woman with her head tilted back, staring straight at her nostrils, then much of the length of her nose disappears from view. You know her nose really is longer than its base, and this is how you continue to draw it, despite what you see. A photograph of her face can help to reinforce the correct proportions, "Look, her nostrils are actually twice as long as the distance between the tip of her nose and her eyebrows." Good visual instincts, or drawing experience, work just as well if not better, but most people find this easier to see in a photo.

I was thirteen when I drew a picture of J.R.R. Tolkien from a black-and-white photo on the dust jacket of one of his books. I reproduced the strange shapes of the shadows on my paper and suddenly there was his unique, pointed nose and his collar faithfully disappearing behind his round neck! In a single step I graduated from dreamy Chagall-inspired faces to a three-dimensional likeness of an individual face. Drawing teachers often discourage their students from working from photos since it doesn't require the same hand-eye coordination. Is it cheating? When David Hockney claimed that many of the old masters used a camera obscura, he created an uproar. (*Secret Knowledge*, 2001, book and television program.) With a camera obscura it is possible to project an image of the painting's subject upside-down onto a sheet of paper or canvas. Literally, they do it

with mirrors. An artist would trace the projection, then carry out the painting with the correct proportions all in place. Whether or not Hockney's theory is true makes no difference here. The importance is that his theory was viewed as a threat to the value of the paintings themselves, reducing their creators to the status of excellent craftsmen.

From my own experience, I have found drawing from photos to be less sensual than drawing from life. The end products can be impressive, yet there is also a danger that an image may become static. It's hard to imagine Cezanne, with his passion for observation, achieving the dynamic overlapping perspectives of his still lifes if he had been working from photos. But for the rest of us mere mortals, there are times when using a photo is helpful.

DRAWING 39, 30" x 22", 1998

Hands are hard to draw. My friend Jane posed for the first drawings of hands. The length of time she could hold the sewing poses was much shorter than the time it took for me to draw them. I made many quick sketches and later continued from memory. Eventually I took snapshots of her hands as she sewed, which gave me the freedom to continue in my own time. The earlier and later drawings of hands show the difference with and without the use of photos (Drawings 9 and 39). But it was also a matter of practice: the more I drew hands, the more skilled I became at drawing them.

Drawing from photos was only a beginning. Like those old maps with dragons swimming in the unexplored edges of the sea, the edges of a photo raise an interesting question: how to proceed from where the photo drops off. In the drawing with many hands (Drawing 39), I combined poses from several photos. I also combined images from separate photos in an unfinished drawing of the scrolls (Drawing 41). If I hung the apron above me, the line made by the bottom of the skirt became most intriguing. I had to crane my neck to see and manipulate this line, and drawing it from below would have been quite uncomfortable, so I photographed it. Unless you already know what you are looking at, the apron in these photos is almost unidentifiable. Many of these images, amorphous floating forms with a delicate, curving line, are beautiful in themselves.

If an image is fully stated in a photo, then why redraw it? Why indeed? I'm not particularly attracted to photographs. I feel overwhelmed by the number of possible moments and the impartiality of the shutter; also the surface of a photograph is so uniform. While I may find individual photographs to be compelling, I rarely seek out a photography show, whereas I love the qualities of a hand-drawn line, the grain of wood in a woodblock print, a stroke of paint, just because I do. I may find that the same subject interests me more when drawn rather than photographed, but that doesn't seem to be enough of a reason to go to the trouble of redrawing a photo. A process of discovery would present a better argument—surprising things may happen as an image is translated from one medium to another—but beyond this, few other creative reasons occur to me. While I was drawing the apron scrolls, my work with the series ended. To all appearances I stopped because of the change in my health, but underlying my question about redrawing these already lovely scroll photos, I can hear a voice quietly declaring that the reason for doing the drawings was coming to its end. It simply happened sooner than I had foreseen.

Everything about an image, starting with the medium, is part of the subject. For example, we know that the Holocaust took place under blue skies as well as gray ones; that in those springs and summers, as the transport trains carried people to the camps like cattle, they passed through green fields filled with wildflowers. The photographs of that time are black and white, and it is easy to conceive of the Holocaust as being in black and white too, for a world without color speaks accurately to our perception of horror. If I had painted the Golden Hands series in brilliant colors, yet made no other changes in the imagery, the meaning would be entirely different.

The way a medium is used also creates a part of the meaning. Imagine looking at a long, dark line on a sheet of paper. If I had pressed the pencil forcefully and moved my arm quickly, leaving a confident, dark stroke, we would register that line differently than we would a line of the same length and tone made in small increments over many hours. Throughout the process of drawing there is an infinite number of possible variations, but once a drawing is finished, we read it only through the marks left on the paper.

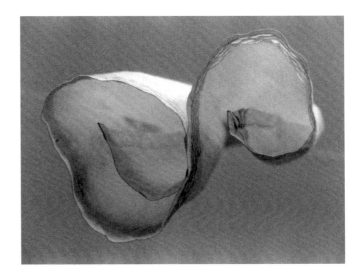

Studies of apron scroll. Photograph. 1998

17

Most often, we register the imagery before anything else. We see an apron, bodies, a violin. If you look at these drawings symbolically, a simple association could be to link the apron to domesticity. Moving past the imagery, light and dark could correspond with good and evil, every shade of gray with nuances of understanding, and layering with the accretion of history. Such marriages of meaning are inescapable— true in part, but equally misleading. The apron was almost transformed into a flower, a ball, or a sail (Drawings 11, 16, and 38), depending on the way I arranged it. An image is elastic. The images I love most, my own or others, are the ones that continue the process of discovery.

The Drawings

The individual Golden Hands drawings have no separate titles. I gave each drawing a number as I started on a fresh sheet of paper. When I completed a drawing, I dated it with the year. I often worked on many drawings simultaneously. I finished some drawings a month or two after I began, while others took up to two years from start to finish. For this reason, the dates of the drawings (as found in the Index, pp. 76–77) don't always follow the same sequence as the drawing numbers.

In the following pages I have arranged the drawings according to the visual movement of the imagery, and they follow a general progression from earlier to later images. They do not appear in a one-two-three order; it isn't how they were done. There are many possible combinations for the order of the images, and as many ways to read them as there are viewer-readers.

Of the total thirty-nine completed drawings, this section reproduces thirty-two. Drawing 42 was adapted for the endpapers. Originally there were forty-two numbered drawings. Drawings 8, 20, and 31 didn't work out, and are not included in the Index.

The drawings are pencil and graphite, 30" x 22". Details are the actual size of the originals.

Drawing 3

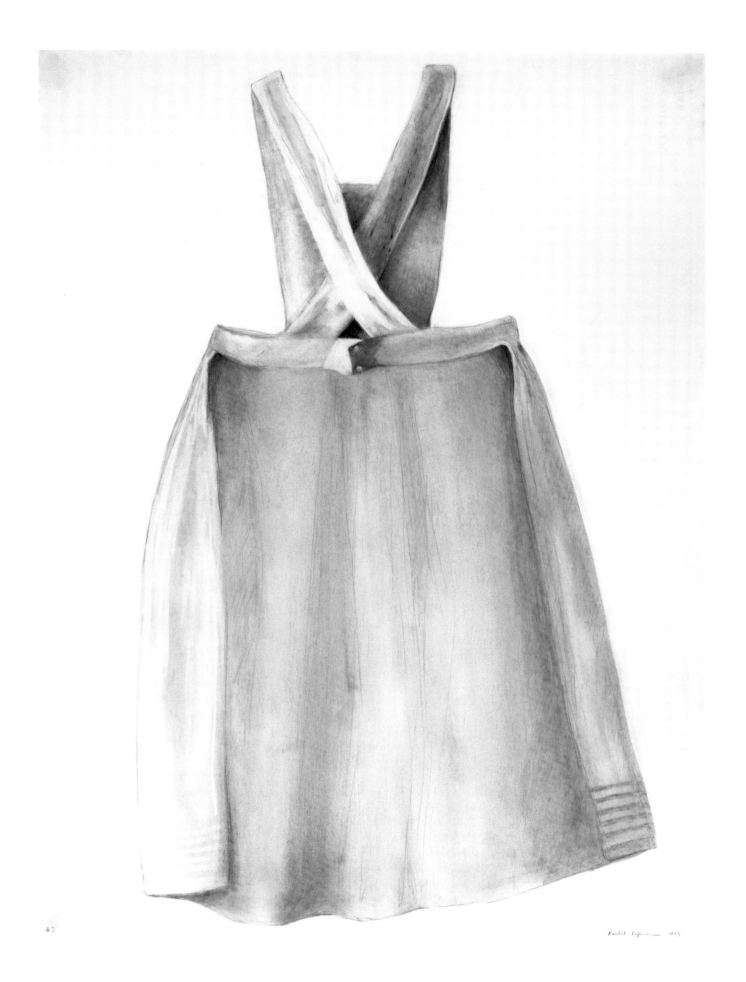

#3   Rachel Hoffman   1979

Drawing 1

Drawing 2 *and detail*

Drawing 4

Drawing 5
On following pages: 2 2 & 6

Arches
FRANCE

#22 Rachel Tiferman 1996

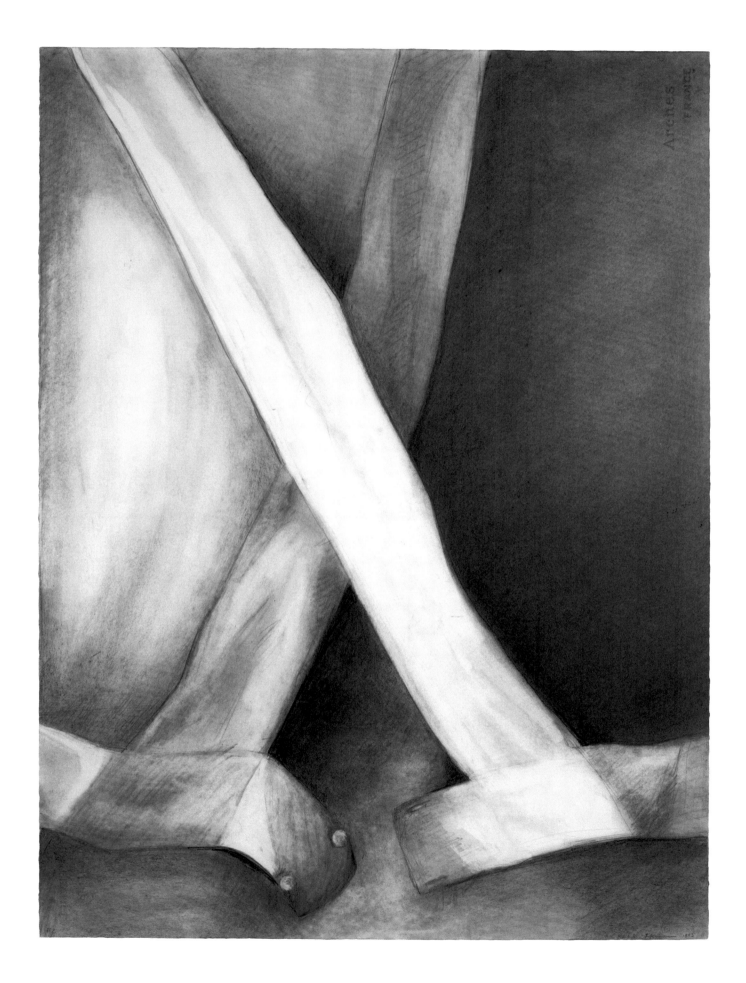

Drawing 7

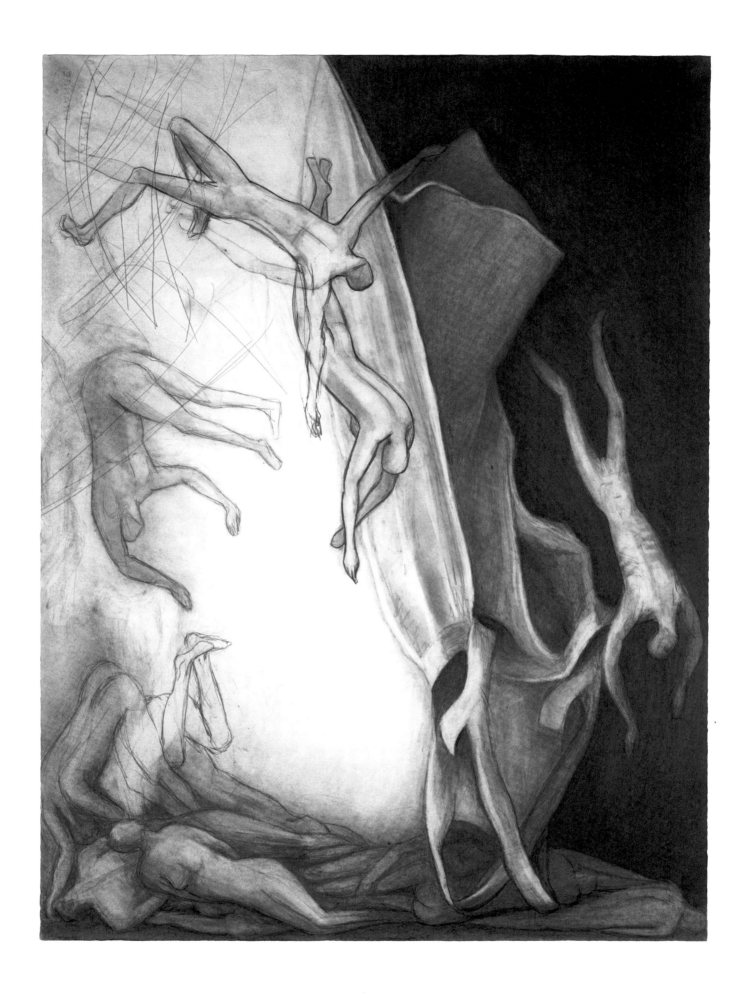

Drawing 9

Drawing 15 *and detail*

Drawing 11

Drawing 13
On following pages: 21 and 16

Drawing 14

Drawing 17

Drawing 33 *and detail*

Drawing 25

#25 Rachel Tulane 1976

Drawing 24
On following pages: 19 and 29

Golden Hands #24   Rachel Freeman 1996

Drawing 27

Drawing 26

Drawing 35 *and detail*

Drawing 36

Drawing 32
On following pages: 28 and 38

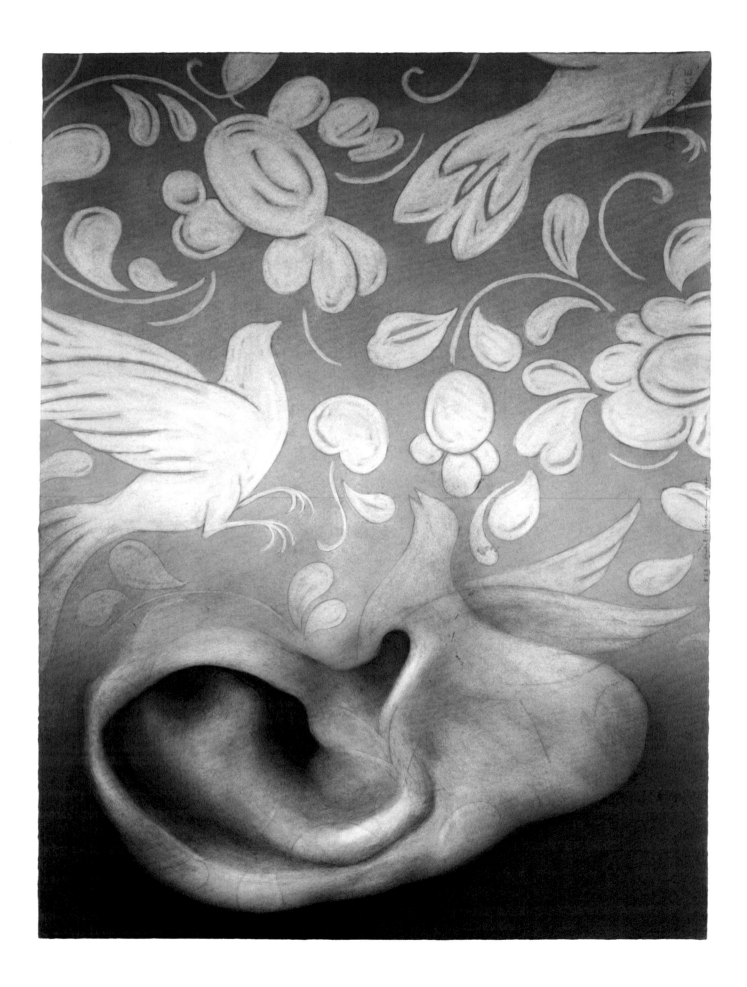

Drawing 30

Drawing 34

Drawing 39

Drawing 40 *and detail*

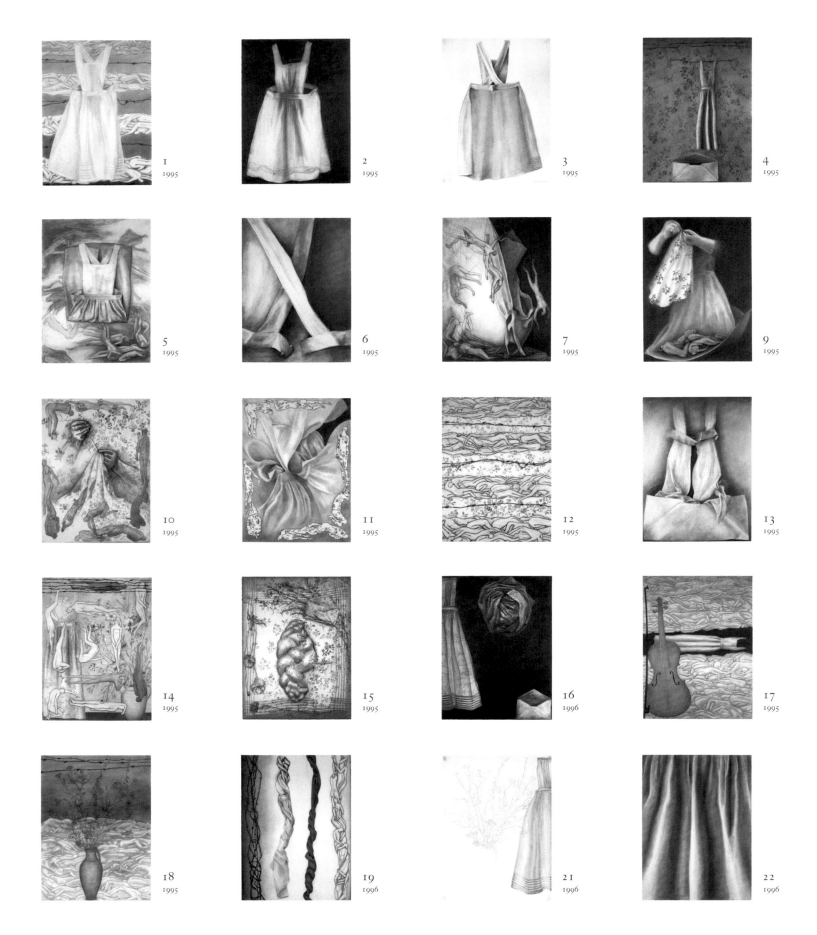

1
1995

2
1995

3
1995

4
1995

5
1995

6
1995

7
1995

9
1995

10
1995

11
1995

12
1995

13
1995

14
1995

15
1995

16
1996

17
1995

18
1995

19
1996

21
1996

22
1996

23
1998

24
1996

25
1996

26
1998

27
1996

28
1997

29
1996

30
1997

32
1996

33
1996

34
1997

35
1996

36
1997

37
1997

38
1998

39
1998

40
1999

41
1999

42
1998

The above sequence does not include numbers 8, 20, and 31, which were never completed.

Rachel and her grandmother Helen

Journal Entries, Dreams, and Letters

The following passages were written during the years I was working on the Golden Hands drawings. The only exception is the first dream from 1993, which belongs with the rest even though it came earlier. The pages of my journals, like the journals of so many others, keep circling around many of the same themes, often with only minimal variations. At the time, I wasn't imagining future readers. Occasionally I have fine-tuned my wording to clarify my original meaning, or condensed a passage to weed out repetition.

When I began the series in 1994, my grandmother Helen was living in a Jewish Home for the Aged in Los Angeles. (She outlived her husband and my maternal grandparents by more than twenty years.) My parents and my sister Julie lived in the San Francisco Bay Area, and I was living in the Pacific Northwest. My grandmother never knew I was working on these drawings and by the time I was ready to share them with her, it was too late. If she were still alive and in her right mind, who knows what she would make of all this.

The distinction between my voice within these journals and my real life is an important one. We are all our own fictional characters, spinning stories about ourselves day and night. When I describe other people, especially members of my family, they are reflected through my eyes, which is not the same thing as who they actually were, or are. The space between life and the mirroring of life becomes even more apparent within my dreams. These dreams left me with unexpected gifts after the tide of sleep had pulled away.

May 8, 1993

Dream: I have a rash on my skin. I'm in a room with overhead lights, I think it is a doctor's office. In order to see the rash clearly, we need to turn off the lights and look at it in daylight. The rash is on the back of my neck, the base of my skull, maybe also on my hands. It's growing in my insides too, like bumps with roots.

When I learn it is skin cancer I double over on the ground. The scene has changed. Now I'm out on the street in front of the hospital. My knees are up against my chest and my head is on the pavement. I find myself staring at the tire of a parked car. I'm crying hard, my heart feels like it's breaking. I say: "I don't want to die, I want to draw!" I mean: I don't want to die without doing a lot more drawing first, and I haven't been doing any.

A doctor in a lab coat comes out to the street because I won't come into the hospital. If I go into the hospital they will give me drugs that might help me get better but would likely leave me unable to draw—at least in the interim. If, instead, I'm at home without drugs, I will be able to draw but will need help. It's implied that the cancer will be fatal, but there are also slender hopes for a remission, through radiation or through drawing. If I draw long enough, hard enough, it may be possible to turn the disease around. There are no guarantees.

I go into the hospital. I have to wear a cone around my neck. I can only be out of bed for three hours each day. During those hours, I draw. I sit cross-legged on a towel on the floor of my hospital room with many small sheets of paper in front of me. I'll work for as long as I can before the side effects of the treatment overtake me.

I want to be at home and to draw there. I want to have my white German Shepherd Jen with me. I'd rather die, or maybe not, at home. At home, I will need my meals prepared and Jen walked. There will be people who can do these daily tasks, but I don't want to visit with anyone, just to draw. I don't even know what is important to draw, perhaps the towers or knots. Just drawing—almost anything—is what matters. I will have to give up my independence in order to do this, and others will make sacrifices. And, if the cancer kills me, I'll have done some drawing first.

It's time for me to check into the hospital. Harriet and I are standing in front of the main entrance. "I always thought it would be me," she says. She hands me a bottle of black ink and a brush. I walk in alone.

April–December 1995

April 1995, from a letter to Muzhe Hacking
  My friend Muzhe had been diagnosed with an aggressive form of cancer. Some photocopies of the first drawings were enclosed with my letter.

I want to share ordinary details and pleasures with you, like the light green of the new leaves on the trees. But most of all, I find I want to share my new drawings with you.

Many years ago, Grandma Helen gave me her white apron, an amazing piece of handwork. You met her a long time ago after Danny's wedding, my little grandmother, and you may remember the apron too, I've had it with my things for a long time. Grandma just turned ninety-eight this week. When I visited her last November, she had changed. I can't always tell the difference between the parts of her stories that are true, but that I've never heard before, and the parts she is imagining.

Just before I visited her, in my class with senior citizens, I had given them an assignment to draw or paint someone important from their past. Four of the women, grandmothers themselves, created pieces about their grandmothers. Two of them painted portraits, the third drew a picture of her grandmother at the kitchen stove with a tethered goat for company, but the fourth found it difficult to draw people. Instead, she painted the tea tray that her Scottish grandmother had brought with her when she came to America. Each image was deeply personal and conjured up a whole way of life that no longer exists.

When I came back home from my visit, with the pictures of the grandmas' grandmas still fresh in my mind, I thought I would like to do some drawings about my grandmother to include in an exhibit at a Jewish Museum in Washington D.C. this summer—a perfect context for Grandma Helen's life. ["From There to Here: Eight Jewish Artists from the Pacific Northwest," B'nai B'rith Klutznick National Jewish

Museum, Washington D.C., 1995.] The idea of creating a portrait through objects opened the door into this work. Since January, I've been drawing the apron and combining it with other things: an envelope, hands sewing, a pattern of flowers, and the dead. It's like a puzzle or a poem, with each picture adding another piece, so the stories keep changing. So far I have fourteen drawings. I just finished five of them before I started this round of teaching on Whidbey.

May 7, 1995

"So you don't tell me the truth."

"Do you know who is talking?"

Grandma is slipping—she's panicked and confused. Somehow from a snatch of a conversation with Dad, Grandma got wind of the fact that I was in California because of an emergency. [I had just come back from visiting my friend Muzhe, who was dying.] Now nothing that we say or write gets through to her.

She believes my sister Julie has died. Why aren't I down there looking after her kids? Which Julie? Is there another Julie? She thinks I'm in a motel in Los Angeles. When will I be coming by? When she registers that I'm at home, she demands to know why, am I just picking up a few things? She's convinced no one is telling her the truth, and since I never tell her anything that would worry her unless absolutely necessary, she's correct. She has no control over this betrayal, no way to get to the truth other than to be convinced of the absolute worst.

Later: "It is probably not even possible for me to formulate those questions which could lead me to radical answers," *Accident*, Christa Wolf. She continues, "The light of language has pushed into the dark entire regions of my inner world which have lain in twilight during pre-language times."

The trap. Bring the subterranean into language, into definition, and lose the grace, the thing itself.

May 13, 1995

The change comes rapidly. I call Grandma last night, on the second try a nurse's aide answers. She tells me she is trying to calm Grandma. I can hear Grandma in the background, crying out the same phrase over and over—maybe something about her glasses. She is inconsolable, like a dog left alone howling.

I speak with my parents, and to my relief they are on their way to go to see her. Dad tells me she fell yesterday and that she is being restrained. The restraints are making her crazy with frustration. I hate to think of her being alone. My work is the link by which I bind myself to her. But I will not get much, if any, drawing done this month.

June 11, 1995

Yesterday I finally managed to return to the drawings. It goes very slowly. Nothing happens. I'm coming away from the demanding work of a teaching residency to the slow grief and craft of these drawings. Just writing about working makes me want to take a nap. The task is to get re-accustomed to the lack of stimulation, then to follow the pull to work as far as it will take me.

Later, rising from a nap. What I mean to say is that the way I work right now is about hitting emptiness, then doing a little more; coming into silence, then picking up again; coming into loneliness, boredom, and, oh yes, into doubts too. It's about persistence. I weave in and out of those states, then dip back into the concentration of drawing.

July 1, 1995

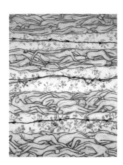

I'm close to resolving thirteen of these drawings and am coming to a turning point—for one thing the dead are becoming their own subject matter. The drawing of the stripes of dead (Drawing 12) doesn't include the apron at all. What other elements are allowed? Challah? A violin? How purely do I want to keep to the apron's story?

I feel weary. Using the dead as a formal design element, void of narrative, is a way to barely tolerate their presence. I would like to break away from these drawings and begin printing huge pictures of bouquets. Bouquets the size of smallish trees in huge vases on four full sheets of BFK. Bouquets for memorial and for celebration. In color.

July 3, 1995

How can I pick this up again? The work is grey and all about loss. I cautiously find my way between two extremes: working hard enough to keep a descent into depression at bay, and working slowly enough—with only half of my attention—so I don't jeopardize my sense of safety.

I've been thinking about the connections between the different visual elements. In subatomic physics, they have found there is all this empty space and infinite possibilities, yet the electron consistently has a tendency to appear in a general area and matter has a tendency to become a physical reality. I latch onto this notion of a tendency—the different elements in my drawings have a tendency to appear together and to form small constellations.

July 19, 1995

Jerry sang two Yiddish songs when our friend Leo was dying. He's a wonderful singer. I asked him if he would teach me the words to "Tum Balalaika." I've wanted to learn this song for at least twenty years. Grandpa Lipa's song. Last night was my first lesson. He took the job very seriously: first we listened to a tape of Yiddish folk songs, and then he went over the pronunciation of each word. Line by line we connected the words with the music. This language that should be mine by inheritance feels clumsy on my tongue. Still, the exhilaration! Afterwards I dreamt that Yiddish words appeared on my screen door and that I had a mezuzah on the doorframe.

October 2, 1995

I was touching up one of the drawings with hands sewing (Drawing 24) and I suddenly saw the reference that has been staring at me all these months: the image of two hands praying. The famous Durer ink drawing, now cliché, of two disembodied hands, with just the shirt cuffs showing.

December 17, 1995

Dream: I'm lying on a pallet on the floor, dying of AIDS. Someone else lay here right before me, someone else will come after. I ask a woman who is with me, "How do your spend your last hour, when you know it's your last hour?" I also say, "I like the character I have been." I'm not in horrible pain, just quiet, my life ebbing. At the end of the hour I die.

Once I have died, or as I'm dying, I see an image of all of us who have died from this disease. Stretched out on our backs, we form a tree of life. Branches come out of our arms and roots come from our feet, linking us to the people on either side. Our bodies become the trunk of each link in this tree-chain. It is life size.

December 25, 1995

I've been trying to figure out a way to incorporate the apron into the drawing of the forest. In the process I find a new pose, the apron lying on the table in a foreshortened view. It looks like it's dancing. I start working with this pose on a sheet already lined with barbed wire and musical notation lines that are made up of thread (Drawing 29). Even if I'm confused about the direction this particular drawing is going, I'm applying a formula that works. As soon as I grasp the fact of this formula, I intuit that I will abandon it in time—predictability will suffocate my interest.

January–December 1996

January 1, 1996

There's a stage near the end of making a Ukrainian egg, when the dyeing is all done and the egg is covered with dark wax, it's greasy and unappealing. This is the point when you begin to work with the egg next to a candle flame, melting the wax lightly, rubbing it with a rag, melting it some more, and gradually your design begins to appear. I taught this to the girls a few weeks ago, they melted, rubbed and then looked—and it looked no different! They were restless and impatient. I took over for them and found I kept stopping to check on the results of each small round of effort too. But that isn't how it gets done. It gets done by paying attention, but not too close attention, and keeping at it. Eventually you hold a glowing, shiny egg with your design.

The same principle applies when I'm drawing—I lose my momentum when I step back to study each change. The longer the pause grows, the harder it becomes to make the effort to draw some more. It's less frustrating to take the vision I can't yet make out on faith and content myself with the pleasure of drawing.

February 20, 1996

Dream: My grandmother's apron is crumpled in front of my face. I see, smell, and taste nothing but the apron. The fabric is worn and dirty with brown spots; it feels crisper than I remember it. I'm breathing and crying into it, though not at the same time. Another woman is on the other side of the apron (my grandmother or mother) breathing back through the apron, and maybe crying into it too. For a brief moment, with my face still burrowed in the apron, I nestle my head in the crook of the other woman's neck. There's a difference between sensing my grandmother and my mother on the other side. With my grandmother the tableau is of me resting against her shoulder and showing her the apron, while with my mother each of us is separately mourning my grandmother's death. It's not an either/or—my mother and grandmother shift back and forth without a clear distinction, for the apron is always between us, keeping us each unseen. Our breath comes up against the soft barrier of the cloth, which partly returns it, a quiet echo, and partly allows it to flow through the tiny holes between threads, mingling it with the breath of the other. All I see is the drapery, all I feel is breath.

March 31, 1996

Sitting with Grandma, holding her hands. In this twilight state, she talks almost entirely with her hands. I think she could hold my hand all day and never tire of it, she draws such comfort from the contact. She feels the skin of my hands. She pulls at my fingers separating each one, starting with the two middle ones. She brings my hand to her lips and kisses it. She moves it to the soft skin of her cheek. Her touch changes all the time. There's the contact that holds tightly, that says, "you're here and I'm never going to let you go" and this newer, more exploratory touch, that seems to be asking, "Whose hand is this?" Or, "What is a hand?" She also uses her hands to tell me what she wants. I'm the third hand, the hand that could do things for her. She moves my hand to the belt strapping her into her wheelchair, to her diaper, to her mouth to indicate she wants a drink, to a wet spot on her shirt, meaning I should dry it. She keeps returning to these same places with the compulsiveness of an animal, her hands fixated on one small concern at a time. Her lack of self-consciousness, so out of character, embarrasses me.

There are other times when she is fully awake and talking. The first evening when her eyes were open, she asked me, "Did you just get off work?" A little later she recognized me, "Rachel! Rachel! Rachel!" She was overjoyed. "You are always on my mind."

When my parents arrived, I was holding her hand. She took my father's hand in her free hand and drew both our hands to her heart. And held them there. She is brimming with the tenderness of the dying. Yesterday, throughout her birthday meal, she sat at the head of the table, blowing everyone silent kisses and occasionally adding, "I love you. I love you all."

The funniest moment was when she woke up at Frieda and Matt's house. She had been in a twilight state all morning and slept through the drive. We despaired, it seemed she might sleep through her birthday party. My sister remembered a nurse once giving her a cup of Sanka in order to wake her up. Someone quickly made a cup of Sanka and it worked like a charm. One by one she saw us, her family and close friends, all gathered around her. "Why are you all here?" she cried out. "Have you made me dead?"

April 16, 1996

I went to see Grandma with the apron washed and pressed, wanting to place it in her hands and to talk to her about making it. But she has drifted too far to be able to tell me her stories. She's left the world of facts; in the drawings, I have as well. What remains here is in our hands, held and known through touch.

May 4, 1996

Evening, after a long walk. Each one of the last drawings has problems I can't solve: the bodies in the woods (Drawing 26), the apron in the case under the violin (33), the large shapes of challah mounds (25), and the delicate drawings of the apron split on the edges of two pieces of paper (16 and 21). I was about to put them all up, when an old photo of Grandma tacked up my bulletin board caught my eye. I was tired, looking for something mechanical to do. I decided to start a drawing of Grandma's face, large (32). This is breaking the rules. The story is to be told through the apron, through inanimate things, and the woman is to be inferred. (The hands are the exception.) And so? The only way I can know if her face belongs with the rest of the images is to try it— I don't have to include it later.

May 9, 1996

Grandma's expression has a sleepiness to it, beauty and plainness too. Her gaze is direct, heartbreaking. As I draw from her photograph, I see my sister on the page, playing through our young Grandma's features. Also my own face, but less so.

June 20, 1996

Ideas for images:
- The apron wrapped around a dead body. Or lying over a pile of bodies.
- The apron in action (how?) on the field of the dead. Breaking through, interrupting.
- How could I show hiding?
- More envelopes, many envelopes. A flood of voices.

July 8, 1996

There's a passage in *The Waves* where Neville says, "Our mean lives, unsightly as they are, put on splendour and have meaning only under the eyes of love." Perhaps this love is more than a personal love but includes our creative expression—what happens, as Virginia Woolf writes, when Schubert composes: "Look! This is the way I can tell you of what I hold most dear." One wouldn't write, or compose, if one didn't have something entirely specific to say. ("What is the phrase for the moon? And the phrase for love? By what name are we to call death? I do not know. I need a little language such as lovers use, words of one syllable such as children speak when they come into the room and find their mother sewing and pick up some scrap of bright wool, a feather, or a shred of chintz. I need a howl; a cry." Again, *The Waves*.)

I weave narratives listening to Schubert, love and death and God and waiting and coming and going and irrevocability and the pounding rage. The intervals between notes and variations over time, sounds like sweeps of color and paint. One art form becomes a metaphor for another, perhaps all art forms are understood the best by the forms they aren't.

July 9, 1996

I seem to lack the motivation to fully solve the problem of earning a living for once and for all. For the equation goes: if I'm successful at earning a living I wouldn't have the time or the right disposition for the work. A middle-aged woman has no need to spend years of her life on pictures contrasting her grandmother's apron with the Holocaust, pairing a female sensibility with the complete annihilation of the earth that we hold dear and not so dear, yet I refuse to give up on this work, hard as it is to keep my hold.

July 15, 1996

A heat wave, spending time in the studio is almost entirely futile. The town is flooded with tourists and I'm having trouble tackling the drawings in any case. How and when I'm able to work, where the work can be shown, whether there is any financial support for it, and whether it will interest anyone, all these things occur in such a slender margin. My faith is at a low ebb.

July 21, 1996

I talked with Julie last night, Grandma is doing worse. More drugged? She had difficulty recognizing Julie and her kids.

November 30, 1996

Dream: I'm walking with my grandmother and three teenage boys. She is able to walk with a person on each side. Our arms are linked, and we form a small procession. It is of unexpected connection, a triumph. The boys get us to a beach. Grandma and I sit turned toward each other, now alone. A gentle wind blows against my face. I say, "It's one thing to go from being human to being just paper, it's a whole other thing to return from paper to being here again." She had been fading. Being paper means being dust, but she's gone through this reversal, from nearly dying to coming outside and here with me once more.

January–December 1997

January 4, 1997

    I wonder if my drawing skill may be pulling me away from the marrow of this work, distracting me from what is tough. It's an arbitrary judgment call: are the pictures more compelling when they are well drawn? Or, does being well drawn create a veneer so seductive that the viewer can merely skim the surface?

February 14, 1997

    Grandma died yesterday afternoon. Julie and I weren't with her at the moment of her death, we had gone to a bookstore for a few hours. We came back to her room and found her. Still, lifeless, not breathing. We sat there with her body, no longer her, for hours. I watched as her skin sank into bones and became waxy. There was no struggle, no agony in her face. When the man finally arrived from UCLA to pick up her body I said good-bye to her for the very last time and kissed her forehead. The feel of this kiss remained on my lips.

    For hours afterwards it was as if I was in the middle of a movie, where it goes from a close-up to a long shot, like what I was looking at was receding farther and farther away, and the whole thing happening at tremendous speed.

    After Grandma died, the nurse on duty called the rabbi. He was on the freeway heading home to Pasadena. He pulled over and called back from his cell phone. He asked if I would like to say the prayers for the dead with him. Yes. I stood holding the phone at the nurses' station and listened to the familiar (but unfamiliar to me) holy words. I cried. The prayer was comforting. He said other absurd and moving things that had no connection with the woman I knew. My parents and grandmother, all atheists, would not have talked to the rabbi, they would have objected to this prayer.

February 18, 1997

    Back home in my studio. My written words are just a companionable chatter side by side with silence, immensity.

February 20, 1997

    All day the waves—yesterday too—have been breaking hard. A cracking rhythm. Big, single waves, not lapping but curling and breaking. Ideas for drawings tumble through me like the incoming tide. This is exciting for it has been a slow eking out of images over the last months.

February 23, 1997

The birdsong was wild at sunrise: a symphony of rejoicing. In the middle of the night I woke up and there was a memory—a palpable sense—of Grandma, just as if she was right there. Instantly I registered my loss as an actual physical loss, a blow. This was so fleeting, her memory-presence slipped away before I could pinpoint anything more.

March 3, 1997

Right after Grandma died, I wanted to spend every available moment in the studio. I would draw until exhausted. There weren't that many available moments—other claims on my time, and the limitations of my body, slowed me down. I completed the two drawings that were close to being finished before she died, the one where she is fading/appearing behind the watery cloth (Drawing 34), and the one of the violin, apples, and apron inside the case (Drawing 36). These two are gateposts; they divide the drawings into the ones that came before her death and the ones still to come.

I enlarged the photos I took of Grandma right after she died, nearly sick to my stomach while doing this, and tacked them up. The photos are just as beautiful as they are horrifying. With her open, gaping mouth she looks like she is singing. The grace of stillness, of surrender.

As long as I was working steadily, though not as much as I desired, I was able to negotiate between her death and my everyday life. Then, half a week ago, I started with dreams. A rash appeared, still here. A reawakened longing and worries about money. All taking me past the point where I'm able to draw, to the place where I consider it a success to accomplish very small things: a walk, a visit, or emptying the compost. I draw comfort from these simple tasks, I can't think ahead. The same inwardness that allows me to transform my feelings into workable material just as easily carries me into depths over my head.

I'm back working again, but no longer with a feverish drive.

Later: There are so few letters from the past. The apron becomes the letter, unfolding before me. The drawings are my long reply.

I'm drawing so slowly that any pretense of a destination is irrelevant. One hundred drawings? Every square inch is dense with pencil, erasing, and more marks. I love this endlessness. It leads nowhere but in.

April 20, 1997

Dream: I'm looking as hard as I can at a bouquet of flowers. I'm trying to memorize them. A voice tells me this isn't necessary. "If, at the moment you're looking, you pay really close attention, that is all that is needed. You will store what you are seeing somewhere inside yourself, within or between your cells, and when you need to see it again it will be there."

I wonder how many people who aren't pledged to some larger work go through this process of weighing: shall I do the laundry, prep a class, tear up the garden to get it ready for bulbs . . . or go to the studio, leaving it all behind? I woke with a quiet feeling, the kind that makes time spent in the studio productive, but by the time I arrive here, the hurrying has done its damage. I'm miles away from inspiration, impatient and irritated instead.

I've been drawing Jane's hands sewing on a page of crosshatching (Drawing 39). The first three pairs of hands lay down beautifully; they matched my preconceived vision of the image, which is unusual. I was tempted to stop after the first pair of hands and again after I added the third pair. Both times the drawing could have been complete. Then came the fourth pair, these hands are foreshortened. I drew the lower hand much too large on my first try. The page looks too crowded, the direction of these hands is downward, and all the others go up. The opposing directions form a diamond shape, this predominates. Have I ruined it? Is there a way to reconcile the parts at odds into a new harmony? It starts to get more interesting.

December 28, 1997, from a letter to Jean Rowlands-Tarbox

It has been a slow fall, my time has been broken up by teaching. Now I'm trying to coax myself back into the habit of drawing and, like a remedial learner, I have to learn to concentrate all over again. I'm working on a complicated pose of Jane's hands threading a needle (Drawing 39) and my rendering feels clumsy. I draw for a minute, or five, or fifteen, then stop to read *Middlemarch*, to eat something, or to stare out the window. Eventually I reapply myself. I have yet to find a means of short-circuiting this—how many times I've been over this same ground I can't tell you—it's so similar to dealing with depression. I've just grown more matter of fact about my slow pace and do my best to resume drawing, as I'm able.

February–December 1998

February 21, 1998

February thirteenth was the anniversary of Grandma's death. For the longest time I've been working on the same three drawings, none of them finished. Some of the work is drudgery, but most of it requires my full attention. I've been holding back on starting any new drawings until these are done, I'm afraid I'd never come back.

The drawings: Grandma as a girl with long hair and a turtleneck sweater standing in front of the woods (Drawing 26). It has many layers of work. First a page of the body pattern, then trees drawn on top of them (done out in the woods at Fort Worden years ago) and lastly, the portrait of Grandma layered on top, so some of the lines of the

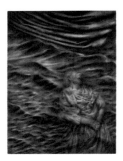

trees too dark to erase are etched in her face. The next one is the portrait of Grandma lying dead against the waves, the apron a dark heavy sail above her (Drawing 38), and last in the series, the drawing of many pairs of hands sewing (Drawing 39). Within each of these, there are areas that don't work. Some of these are places where I didn't have visual information to refer to: no photo of the edge of Grandma's gown or forgetting what the light was like on the trees, so it's guesswork each time I draw these. When I start changing one area, it sets off a string of adjustments—every part of a picture is relative to every other part.

March 13, 1998

Mourning. Lamentation. Immobility.

March 28,1998

I'm bringing the three drawings to an arbitrary close since I decided I wanted to have slides of them for upcoming proposals. When is a drawing finished? I can't tell if all the work has made them that much better than in earlier stages. I've been holding onto these pictures for reasons beyond their quality— the year of mourning.

April 9, 1998

One day last week I came in and cleaned the studio. Put away work, re-papered the tables. A lingering cold and depression lifted Tuesday.

For the last year I've always had drawings in process, the only question was which piece to work on. Today I have choices. There are two pages of patterns—the bodies in dark lines and the pattern of the pitcher—up on the wall. I've been working on a grant application, more to follow. For the business side of my artwork, I become a secretary, marketer, and writer. When I come to back to drawing, I'm stripped of language. Those roles only get in my way.

June 13, 1998

The day before I left to teach a drawing workshop at the Coupeville Arts Center, my submission materials were returned from The Drawing Center with the shortest of rejection letters, nothing personal or encouraging. I had labored on this application and cried hard when I read it.

Then, when I came back home, there was a personable letter from Ed Cain asking if I would be interested in putting a small number of drawings in a show at his gallery in August. The tone of his letter warms me. Recognition comes in small increments, a little more of the same.

June 29, 1998

I read something about the Torah scroll and thought: what if the side of the apron curled to mimic a Torah? I couldn't figure out how to see the scrolling until I hung the apron above me. I saw just what I wanted and took photos. I don't know how I will use them but my excitement is like the first good rain after a drought.

July 2, 1998

Ed Cain came back to look at drawings in my studio. He was going to pick a couple of the drawings for his upcoming exhibit, "The Human Form." As he looked through them again, he decided he would like to feature a selection of ten to twelve of the aprons in the back room. I kept pulling out more work. By the time he left, he wanted to put up as many of them as he could—so over the course of an hour I'm staring at the possibility of a one-person show, buzzing with excitement.

July 19, 1998

Dream: I'm writing a letter on a huge pad of paper, like newsprint, the sheets are taller than my body, and just as wide. My words are black, in script. The pressure of the pen etches my words into the sheet beneath. Maybe the words are from the past, like a manuscript, or maybe the letter is written in Russian and will be mailed from Russia. A letter could go instantly by email, but it's important that this piece of paper move from one physical place to another, that the pressure of the pen leaves its trace, and that the person receiving this letter holds these same dark-shaped words.

September 18, 1998
The exhibition at the Ed Cain Galleries, Port Townsend, Washington, was up during September.

I don't remember other shows of mine exerting such complete influence over me. It is fixed in the center of my mind and seems to be going on almost indefinitely. My life won't re-adjust until it's over—only a long week from now. Every night while I sleep, I'm aware of the room with the image of the apron repeating, and where every single drawing is hanging. The work—it is still a living thing in my psyche, not yet complete.

September 29, 1998

I woke feeling lighter than I have for weeks. Within less than two hours I left the rooms in the gallery empty; the show is down.

Ed was working on the poster for the next show, Ann Hirondelle's ceramic forms. The brighter star; the endless rotation. Jealousy and relief and a return to ordinary days—I'm immediately back into a full fall teaching schedule.

October 10, 1998

I dream: My airplane lands, I'm walking from the runway to the airport carrying a millipede in a glass jar, preserved in formaldehyde. My friends Victor and Linda C. are waiting for me. As I approach Victor says, "Rachel, life has given you millipedes, earthworms, slugs, all these small creatures that disgust you so, to study and protect—

isn't it a paradox!" I'm thinking about what he has said, when I realize he's just spoken a clear sentence. [In waking life Victor had suffered a severe stroke and lost his fluency with words.] "Victor! You've got your tongue back!" We laugh and laugh.

January–May 1999

January 26, 1999

With the laundry done, I headed over to the Chinese Gardens. The light of the setting sun was reflected in the moving water of the pond. Suddenly, under this dome of clear sky after days of clouds and wind, I felt like one of the luckiest people alive.

I've been drawing small negative spaces between twigs (Drawing 40) for days. Working dark on dark, it's hard to see what I'm doing. Away from the drawing, I'm noticing new things, greedily storing away the shapes and colors that please my eye. I imagine that I'll be turning to painting soon. Beauty is scattered throughout these days. The light has already begun lengthening—spring is coming.

May 10, 1999

After months of not drawing, followed by several months of eking out this drawing of the apron on the ground—which I like, but is a strain to pull off—ideas for pictures are flowing again. My ability to concentrate for long stretches has returned. I'm working with curling nestling shapes (Drawing 41). I'm excited by the imagery and energized by the excitement itself. I walk into the studio and think: this is where I want to be.

Epilogue

The Garden, October 2007

The crabapple tree is covered with little red crabapples, just like the ones that were pictured on its tag. We've planted many trees this year and I still wish to put in more. I'd like to plant a coral bark maple in the spot where the red currant died, so I can see a glow of red branches against the blue wall of the studio in the winter. I had hoped to get the long bed that runs alongside the walk turned over, and the plants in pots tucked into the ground before winter comes. This last seems the most achievable. The forsythia and the dark blue ceanothus, gifts from last year, are already planted. Chilling tulips fill two shelves of the refrigerator, while crocuses, daffodils, and alliums are all ready to be buried. Then I wait for spring to see if the promise holds.

Over the last year I've been putting in a garden. With ongoing help from my family, friends, neighbors, and gardeners, the weed-filled plot of hard dirt is being transformed into a sanctuary enclosed between my house and my studio. I've been working on this book over the same stretch of time. Books and trees and the end of one's life—they all connect. I recently dreamt of a hand-drawn book of trees. A woman sitting inside a cart, which was at the center of a small procession, had created it. It was exquisite. On every page of the book was a tree and every part of every page was completely filled. I think about my friend Jon Ericson, and how, during the year before he died of AIDS, he photographed many trees. One of these photos, of an old copper beech tree, hangs above my couch where I see it often. The bulk of this tree, with its large circle of roots, comforts me.

I had never planted a tree of my own until now. To plant a tree is to place a foothold in the future, even if we no longer take this future for granted. The first thing many people do when moving into a new home is to rip up the garden (along with the carpet) in order to make it their own. Bleaker souls also factor in the possibility of the end of the world, or a world changed beyond our recognition. I hope that the trees we've planted shall continue to grow for many years to come. I imagine a sheltering canopy of big leafy branches arching over the pathway to the front door, with the sound of song birds coming from above, but this dream is also held in the moment—my book is finished and my garden keeps growing.

Afterword by Linda Brownrigg

I first met Rachel Feferman in the mid 1970s. I had been invited to the home of her parents, Solomon and Anita Feferman, and in their stunning wood and glass house I admired a wall of large windows covered by colorful and sophisticated batik shades with designs of animals and birds. Rachel, then age twenty, had designed and made them. I too lived in a wood and glass house, and invited Rachel to make shades for my bedroom and over time for other windows as well. For some thirty years I have awakened to see the images of horses and birds, trees and flowers, in blues and greens and purples, framed as though in a manuscript illustration, which was my Ph.D. study focus and her inspiration. The colors have not faded.

I collect work by artists who work in clay, textiles, wood, and glass. My home has work by Rachel in every room and in many media. Daily, by the front door, I meet Joe, a laconic figure, seated, a three-foot soft sculpture dressed in pink plaid trousers and a patterned shirt, a rather sour expression on his sewn leather face, wearing a blue cap, now sitting with his arm around a vase but for decade or two reading a bit of the *Financial Times*. In the kitchen I enjoy a blue and white coffee pot—four plump and very individual women dance around the circumference. It is one of a series of blue-and-white ceramic ware Rachel decorated when working with her potter partner Jane Stein, and by the same pair there is a teapot with cheerful faces looking out of a window, and a plate with a girl reading. In my desk there are correspondence cards I won't part with, Rachel's pen and ink drawings of persimmons, of California quail perching one on top of another.

These drawings are from the late 70s, a transitional time for Rachel. On the one hand, she continued to produce saleable art, but around the time she received her BFA from Lone Mountain College in San Francisco, she completed a series of more personal dream-like (or nightmare-like) pen-and-ink drawings.

When I visited her in her tiny studio at the top of the President Hotel in Palo Alto shortly before she moved to the Northwest, she had begun painting with gouache. The 1980s were a fraught time: the news from Central America was full of horror and death. When Rachel moved to Seattle in the mid-1980s her new work, in graphite and gouache, turned to dark themes (some had been present in her soft sculpture, though Joe is benign). This work found a larger audience; it was represented by Davidson Galleries in Seattle (between 1989 and 1994), shown in juried exhibitions in Washington State, as well as in the National Museum of Women in the Arts, and the B'nai B'rith Klutznick National Jewish Museum, both in Washington, D.C.

Rachel's making from the 70s, her craft and its spirit, has been an ever-present source of emotional and visual pleasure in my life. But in the late 1980s, when Rachel finished a series of gouache paintings, I was brought up short. Her work had become political and painful. I could see the point: this was a very hard time; we knew about the suffering in Nicaguara and El Salvador, to which I thought the images might be referring. But her pencil and graphite images were unsparing. From an exhibition I bought one, perhaps the least demanding, which shows what can be understood as healing and reconciliation, a circular composition with a tree of life in the center, and figures passing along concentric circular passages carrying bodies, others walking on crutches. But the violent and yet beautiful "Hole in the Heart #1," two women in a circle, men with guns, vivid with one woman's red blood, has stayed with me. Hard to live with but unforgettable. I think of Goya.

      That brings me to the images in this book. I knew Rachel's grandmother; we shared the same birthday and I joined the family for a celebration not very many years before Helen died. Rachel's journal entries around the time of her grandmother's death resonate with me. (The rabbi, pulling off the freeway to say prayers for an atheist, and Rachel's acceptance.) But my commitment to this book began when I saw the portrait drawing of her grandmother that Rachel gave to her parents in the 1990s. I was astonished by it. And then I learned there were many more.

      I immediately felt that these drawings, and at the time I only knew a few, deserved a wider audience than friends and family. I have come to know them better over the months of producing this book, learning about how they were made, and over how many years. "In the Studio" is a crucial introduction to Rachel's complex process of layering, which will bring the viewer to look closely at each image. Each is remarkable. The means so simple: black and white, graphite and erasers, and the result so rich. We learn how the imagery that accompanies the apron in its many guises is related to Rachel's choices of subject and her life in Port Townsend, Washington—the barbed wire that recalls the Holocaust is drawn from a piece found in a nearby field; a pitcher in a friend's kitchen is chosen to hold flowers for the dead. The Journal section opens the door into Rachel's dreams, and allows us to watch her in her life, working through problems, whether in the ongoing history of her love for her grandmother or how to earn a living or organize an exhibition. The text provides an unusual insight into an artist's life, and how life becomes art, not in a novel, but in graphite on paper. The drawings speak for themselves.

Acknowledgments

It was a privilege to have the time to create these drawings and then to write about them.

A very special thanks to Linda Brownrigg, publisher, for making this book possible, and to Jaime Robles, editor, designer, and production manager, for turning it into a reality. Thanks also to Terry Reed for fine digital photography work. Each brought a loving attention to the project that comes through on every page.

Gratitude to Harriet Sanderson and Peggy Smith Venturi for conversations about the drawings when I was doing them, to Jane Mitchell for unwavering faith, and to the late Ed Cain for showing the drawings in progress. For belief in this work, thanks to Deborah Walker, Marc Wenet, Inge Norgaard, Stephen Yates, Carole Eversole Yates, Jean Rowlands-Tarbox, and Patricia Burbank. For reading earlier drafts, Barbara Arrn, Linda Chrisman, and for catching countless mistakes, Rima Phillips.

Even if Miss Chute, my seventh grade art teacher, had not raved about the joie de vivre in my paintings, the arrow of my compass was already swinging north. However, as is the case with all the best teachers, her interest stimulated my sense of direction. A special thanks to Michael Spafford for challenging my thoughts about art during one year of graduate study at the University of Washington in 1989; the seeds planted then would lead me to find the form for these drawings years later. Thanks also to my students who—to my delight—continued to educate me while they themselves learned to draw and paint.

For the other women I know who live with cancer, and also those who have died, my deepest appreciation. The shared uncertainty, heartbreak, and humor too, have made it a little easier to bear. Heartfelt gratitude as well to many nurses and doctors for expertise and kindness when it really matters, and to Dr. Ann E. Murphy for these years.

There isn't enough space to name each friend who has made a difference during this time. I remain touched by everyone who has been able to say yes along the way. Yes, I will come visit. Yes, I can go with you to a doctor's appointment. Yes, I am able to listen. Yes, I can walk the dog. Yes, I will help with the housework. These gifts of friendship and community have sustained me.

Loving thanks to Cynthia Broshi who said "Write it for me," and to Michael Van Horn and Patty Wittmann for being there. Hours spent together—and also with others dear to me—looking at art, cooking delicious meals, commenting on the arrival of the hummingbirds or the progress of the pale yellow peonies, have nourished my soul.

Lastly, with much love, I gratefully acknowledge my family: my sister, Julie Feferman; my nieces, Ysabel and Graciela Feferman-Perez; my parents, Solomon Feferman and Anita Burdman Feferman; and their parents, Lipa and Nellie Burdman, and Leon and Helen Feferman, who each made the long journey to a new world.

This book was designed and typeset by
Jaime Robles. The type is Janson. The
book and cover are printed on archival
Mohawk Superfine. Terry Reed digitally
photographed the artwork and processed
the files for use in this book. The book
was printed at Autumn Press in Berkeley,
California. The book is bound in Iris cloth
by Taurus Bookbindery, San Francisco.